Animal Activities

KEEPING COOL

JANE BURTON

For a free color catalog describing Gareth Stevens' list of high-quality children's books call 1 (800) 433-0942

Editors' Note: The use of a capital letter for an animal's name means that it is a species of animal (for example, a Leopard Tortoise). The use of a lowercase, or small, letter means that it is a member of a larger group of animals.

Library of Congress Cataloging-in-Publication Data
Burton, Jane.
     Keeping cool / by Jane Burton; photography by Jane Burton and Kim Taylor. -- North American ed.
       p. cm. -- (Animal activities)
       Includes index.
       Summary: Describes how animals stay cool in hot weather, by such actions as wallowing in mud, burrowing, or panting.
       ISBN 0-8368-0188-1
       1. Body temperature--Regulation--Juvenile literature. 2. Adaptation (Physiology)--Juvenile literature. 3. Animals--Juvenile literature. [1. Body temperature--Regulation. 2. Animals--Habits and behavior.] I. Taylor, Kim, ill. II. Title. III. Series: Burton, Jane. Animal activities.
QP135.B87   1989b
599'.01912--dc20   89-11412

This North American edition first published in 1989 by

Gareth Stevens Children's Books
7317 W. Green Tree Road
Milwaukee, Wisconsin 53223, USA

Format copyright © 1989 by Gareth Stevens, Inc. Supplementary text copyright © 1989 by Gareth Stevens, Inc. Original text copyright © 1989 by Jane Burton. Photographs copyright © 1989 by Jane Burton and Kim Taylor. First published in Great Britain in 1989 by Belitha Press Ltd.

Editors, U.S.: Patricia Lantier and Valerie Weber

Printed in the United States of America

1 2 3 4 5 6 7 8 9 95 94 93 92 91 90 89

Animal Activities

KEEPING COOL

JANE BURTON

Gareth Stevens Children's Books
MILWAUKEE

All animals are uncomfortable when they are too hot. There are many ways that they can get cool and keep cool.

The Common Toad hides in damp places in the daytime and comes out only at night. It stays cool all the time.

This Leopard Tortoise loves warmth, but if it gets too hot, it paddles in a puddle to cool itself.

In hot countries, the early morning and the evening are pleasant and warm, but in the middle of the day, the sun can be scorching. Then, animals rest in the shade.

A tall thorn tree spreads its branches like an umbrella, making a sunshade for two Giraffes. They doze away in the midday heat. Keeping still helps them to keep cool.

A Rock Hyrax shelters in the shadow of some boulders. When the sun goes down, the hyrax will scamper out to feed.

Cats hate the cold and love warmth, but they can also suffer from the heat. On a very hot day, Septimus creeps into the log pile, panting. It is cooler in the shade, and panting cools him too.

Lions always look really uncomfortable in the middle of the day, especially after they have had a big dinner. This African Lion spent most of the day trying to keep cool under a little bush. In the evening, still panting, he has come out to wait for his next dinner.

Mammals in cold countries have long, shaggy coats of thick fur to keep out the cold. In hot countries, they have fine, pale fur. Zebu are graceful cattle with pale coats and dark eyes. They live in hot countries. Light-colored coats reflect the sunshine, so that the sun's heat mostly bounces off their backs. A Grant's Gazelle buck stays out even at midday. His back shines as it reflects the sunlight.

Tess is not happy on the beach in the summer. Her black coat soaks up the sun, and she soon gets too hot. She squeezes into a narrow strip of shade, trying to get out of the sun. The white rocks feel cool because they reflect the sun, and the pebbles are cold and damp to lie on.

Mud on the skin is cooler than water, which dries up quickly. Mud holds dampness longer and protects skin from the sun.

Elephants love to wallow. They suck up muddy water with their trunks and squirt it all over themselves. This African Elephant lives where the mud is red. In other places, the mud may be a different color, but it is still good for cooling off!

The earth is brown where this Kongoni lives. It has been raining, so there is mud everywhere. The Kongoni rubs his face and horns in the mud, then gnaws at an itch.

A stag spikes at the mud with his antlers. Wallowing in mud makes him feel good and smell great!

Hippopotamuses have thick skin. It looks tough, but they can still suffer from sunburn. So to keep cool and to avoid getting sunburned, they spend the whole day in the river. They can swim nimbly under water, but most of the time, they laze just below the surface.

The Pygmy Hippopotamus is smaller and lives in streams in the forest. All hippos come on land in the evening to eat grass. They graze like lawn mowers all night while it's cool.

When an animal is hot, it gets cool by losing moisture from its body. Many mammals have special glands for this, called sweat glands, in their skin. The sweat glands ooze water droplets that evaporate into the air, cooling the skin. Tag has been playing with his brother. He stretches and pants in the shade, trying to cool off.

Jasper has been romping with Tess. He flops down under the garden chair, sweating and panting so hard that he froths at the mouth.

Foxes and dogs cool themselves by panting. They have sweat glands only in their feet. Horses have sweat glands all over. When a horse runs, its coat gets wet with sweat. Percy the foal is dozing in the sun. His coat is dry now.

In the hot dry season, animals get very thirsty, just from losing moisture through their skin and their breath. They must drink every day to put back into their bodies the water they have lost in keeping cool.

Some thirsty Warthogs come to a water hole in the early morning. After a long drink, they will wallow in the mud. Pigs are like dogs; they only sweat through their feet, not all over their body. They need the damp mud on their skin to keep them cool while they feed in the sun.

The water hole is busy with animals coming and going. Impalas drink their fill and then move away. Two elands come with Red-billed Oxpeckers on their backs. When the big antelope drink, the birds will sip.

Most of the large mammals leave the water hole as soon as they have had enough to drink. Lions or a leopard could be lying in wait in any of the nearby bushes. The smaller birds also drink, then fly away. Only the big Marabou Storks stay behind, resting and preening.

In the rainy season, a Leopard Tortoise finds green plants to eat and puddles to drink and wallow in. But when the hot dry season starts and greenery and puddles disappear, the tortoise also disappears — into the earth to keep cool for the rest of the year.

When the desert sand gets baking hot, the Pink-tailed Lizard stands on two feet at a time — back left, front right — and holds the other two feet up to cool them. Then it changes feet, standing on the back right and front left, and cools the first two feet.

In the midday heat, the Kori Bustard is on its way to a water hole. It glances up to watch an eagle soaring in the sky. The bustard is panting to keep cool. Its feathers are flat so that the heat from the sun bounces off them.

Black fur absorbs heat and white fur reflects heat. Does the zebra feel hot and cold in stripes — or just warm all over? A Burchell's Zebra yawns, not because it's sleepy but as an extra way of trying to keep cool.

In the desert, it is scorching hot in the daytime but quite cool at night. It is also cool underground. Many small animals keep cool by staying beneath the surface during the day and coming out after dark.

The tiny desert gerbil digs itself a deep burrow in the sand. It sleeps underground in the day and comes out to eat seeds during the night.

The large scorpion makes its burrow beneath a big stone. It emerges only after sundown.

Ears act as radiators — they give out heat. The heat of a mammal's body is carried in its blood into the veins in its ears. Some of the heat in the blood goes out through the bare skin into the air, making the animal cooler.

Many of the mammals that live in hot places have big ears for keeping cool. You can often tell from the size of its ears whether an animal lives where it is hot, cold, or in between. The Fennec Fox is a little desert fox with enormous ears. Arctic Foxes have small ears, and Red Foxes have middle-sized ears. The blood vessels in the Belgian Hare's ears look like the veins of a leaf.

A big body is good at staying warm, and it is harder to cool than a little body. The African Elephant is the largest land animal in the world, and so he has a big problem keeping cool. Under the hot midday sun, he needs to lose a lot of heat from his great bulk.

To help it get rid of the extra heat, the elephant's ears are also huge. As he tramps through the bush, he fans and flaps his ears. They make quite a wind, which blows heat away and helps the elephant to keep cool.

Fun Facts

1. Tigers in the jungle often lie in the water to cool off when the tropical heat gets too intense.

2. The body temperature of a camel changes. It falls during the cold night and then slowly rises during the day. This way the camel avoids over-heating during much of the day.

3. A bird called the Laysan Albatross tries to cool off by holding its feet off of the hot ground. Heat radiates from the exposed skin on its feet.

4. Pigs like to keep cool by taking luxurious mud baths!

5. Elephant Seals throw damp gravel or sand over themselves to cool off.

6. A bird called the Egyptian Plover sprinkles river water on its eggs to cool them.

7. A jackrabbit's long ears help it lose body heat; a bat's wings do the same for it.

8. Tiny desert shrews in Mexico hide in grass nests to avoid intense heat.

9. There are about two-and-a-half million sweat glands on an adult's body!

For More Information About Animal Life

These books and magazines will tell you many interesting things about animals. When possible, we have listed videos. Check your local library or bookstore to see if they have these materials or will order them for you.

Books:

About Animals. Scarry (Western)
African Animals. Purcell (Childrens Press)
All About Animals. Gregorich (School Zone)
Animals of the African Plains. Cuisin (Silver Burdett)
Animals Underground. Ruffault (Young Discovery Library)
Desert Animals. Carwardine (Scholastic)
Hidden Animals. Leslie (Dial Books for Young Readers)
How Animals Live. Civardi and Kilpatrick (EDC)
In the Jungle. Booth (Raintree)

Magazines:

Chickadee
Young Naturalist Foundation
P.O. Box 11314
Des Moines, IA 50340

Owl
Young Naturalist Foundation
P.O. Box 11314
Des Moines, IA 50340

National Geographic World
National Geographic Society
P.O. Box 2330
Washington, DC 20013-9865

Ranger Rick
National Wildlife Federation
8925 Leesburg Pike
Vienna, VA 22184-0001

Videocassette:

Animals in Spring and Summer. (Encyclopaedia Britannica Educational)

Things to Do

1. Find out the difference between a *sunburn* and a *sunstroke*. Write a definition for each and then explain the best way to treat these heat-related problems.

2. Find out how wearing light-colored clothing in summer helps to keep us cool. Are there certain types of fabric or material that are cooler than others?

3. Make a list of your favorite cool summer drinks and snacks.

4. Draw and color a picture of yourself in what you would consider a terrific place to keep cool in the heat of summer.

5. What types of clothes do *you* wear in summer? Describe your typical summer wardrobe.

Things to Talk About

1. Discuss with a teacher or a parent some of the dangers of being too warm or too hot. What are some of the medical problems that can result from too much heat?

2. Many animals sweat when they are too warm. This helps them to cool off. Try to remember the last time you began to sweat after playing or working hard. Did sweating help you to feel cooler? Why or why not?

3. Some animals stay cool by sleeping during the hot daytime hours and coming out only in the cool of night. How does this plan sound to you?

4. Why do you think keeping still can help to keep you cool?

5. Do some of the foods you eat in summer differ from those you eat in winter? Why? Discuss the types of foods you eat more often in each season.

6. Why is water such a super "cooler"? How does bathing help to cool the skin? Why is drinking a lot of water a healthy habit?

7. Why do so many people seem to consider the beach an ideal place to keep cool even though sandy beaches are hot and the sun is sizzling?

8. Discuss the sun's ultraviolet rays and their effect on people. What are doctors and scientists warning us to do if we want to go out in the sun?

9. Discuss the many different ways human beings try to keep cool during the hottest months of summer. Ask other friends and your parents for additional ideas.

Glossary of New Words

antlers: the branched horns on the head of deer.

boulder: any large rounded rock.

burrow: a hole or tunnel dug in the ground by an animal.

creep: to move along slowly.

doze: to nap; to sleep lightly; to be half-asleep.

emerge: to come out into full view; to appear.

evaporate: to change from a liquid or a solid into a vapor; to vanish.

foal: a baby horse; a young horse.

froth: a white mass of bubbles, or foaming saliva.

gnaw: to chew on or bite with the teeth.

graze: to feed on growing grass, as in a field or pasture.

laze: to loaf; to spend time idly.

mammals: any of a large class of hairy, warm-blooded animals whose babies feed on their mother's milk.

nimble: moving or acting quickly and lightly.

pant: to breathe rapidly and heavily.

preen: in relation to birds, to clean and smooth feathers with the beak.

reflect: to throw back light, heat, or sound from a surface.

romp: to play in a lively manner.

scorch: to parch, shrivel, or spoil by heat that is too intense.

sweat glands: special glands in animals that give off sweat in an effort to keep the body cool.

wallow: to roll about in mud, dirt, or water.

Index